7 DANZAS CUBANAS TIPICAS
(Seven Typical Cuban Dances)
for PIANO

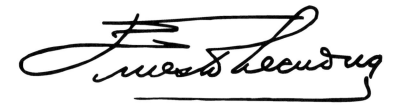

Arranged by
Thomas Y. Tirino

ISBN 978-0-634-01383-6

EDWARD B.
MARKS MUSIC
COMPANY

EXCLUSIVELY DISTRIBUTED BY

7777 W. BLUEMOUND RD. P.O. BOX 13819 MILWAUKEE, WI 53213

Visit Hal Leonard Online at
www.halleonard.com

PREFACE

The piano works of Ernesto Lecuona have no category or limitations. Composing over 175 pieces for piano, Lecuona wrote a great body of piano literature that is just beginning to be rediscovered. In preparing this, the first completely new edition of Lecuona's piano music in more than 30 years, it is important to realize the position of the maestro's compositions in serious classical repertoire, and to address its maximum impact on the musical community of the world. Owing much to Cuba's rich heritage, Lecuona's music transcends the past, and is reborn as fresh music for a new millenium.

The piano music of Ernesto Lecuona is a hybrid of many different structures and sonorities melded together to create new forms and sounds. The principal characteristics are beautiful melodic lines, woven around powerful Spanish, native Cuban, and Afro-Cuban rhythms. However, Lecuona's color palette and harmonic frameworks are not limited by these forms. Touches of French impressionism and 19th century European romantic music are often found within his style. The universality of Lecuona's prodigious gifts comes full circle with references at times to particularly American influences. As Lecuona and Cuba's past were cosmopolitan, the composer's music equally reflects the global experience that was the history of Cuba. The combination of these musical elements gives his works a wide mass appeal and popularity for performers and audiences everywhere.

Ernesto Sixto de la Asunción Lecuona y Casado was born August 6, 1895 in the village of Guanabacoa, Cuba, across the bay from Havana, and died November 29, 1963 in Santa Cruz de Tenerife in the Canary Islands. He was the dominant force in Cuban music for many years, enjoying an international career that extended even to Hollywood. Lecuona composed his first work at age 11, his first song at age 18, and by the age of 24 wrote his first musical score for the esteemed theater revue, *Domingo de Piñata*. He had a brilliant career as a distinguished concert pianist performing standard classical repertoire. Beginning piano studies with his sister Ernestina, and continuing with Carreras, Saavarda, Nín and Hubert de Blanck, he had a powerful left hand, and his music reflects this virtuosity. His piano works and his song accompaniments, in their original forms and *tempi*, demonstrate the need for an accomplished pianist to play the pieces properly and according to the composer's wishes.

Lecuona made many recordings for RCA and Columbia records, as well as numerous piano rolls for Ampico, Duo Art, and other piano roll companies. After 1932, he concentrated on composing and performing his own compositions. It is a great legacy of art left to us.

This volume of *Siete Danzas Cubanas Típicas* is the first publication ever of these works in their original form. They represent a small sample of what is available among the compositional treasures of Lecuona. It is indeed fitting then, that these, some of the composer's most important piano works, illuminate the public to the richness that is Cuba, through the genius that was Lecuona.

Thomas Y. Tirino
October 21, 1999

INTRODUCTION

The *danza* is more than just a dance: it is a particular musical form from Cuba. Its origins are in the *contradanza,* brought to Cuba in the 18th century by the Spanish, who took it from the French. The *danza* fuses Spanish melody, African rhythms, and the choreographic structure of the French ballroom *contradanse.* A *danza* is rapid, full of joy, and danced independently by couples. Traditionally in binary (A-B) form, and in 2/4 time, it has a second half in sharp contrast to the first, usually quicker, or different in character and mood. This is important to remember when performing Lecuona's *danzas. Tempi* are quite fast, (as demonstrated in Lecuona's own earlier recordings of the works) and should *not* be performed slowly or lugubriously, as it would render the form itself ludicrous. They require great dexterity and virtuosity, and are at times like miniature études. The *danzas* represent Lecuona's greatest compositional achievements for the piano. A unique contribution to music, Lecuona was one of the firsts to pioneer the introduction of Afro-Cuban form and rhythms into the concert hall.

The *Siete Danzas Cubanas Típicas* were not composed as a set, but rather as separate works between 1920-1925, during the period that Lecuona wrote two other great bodies of *danzas,* featured in the volumes *Danzas Afro-Cubanas* and *Danzas Cubanas.* This represents the third and last body of pieces in that style, compiled into a collection by the composer in 1950. (*La Comparsa* and the *19th Century Danzas* however, were written before 1920). Though the composer used the form beyond 1925, *El Miriñaque* was the last *danza cubana* written for piano solo.

 A unique problem in playing the music of Lecuona is which version of a work to use. Lecuona's performing and compositional styles were improvisatory, and often what was a published edition was merely a guide with directions for the whole conception of the composer. To complicate this, Lecuona made revisions of manuscripts and works along the years, and recorded his works differently as well. Certain fluidity of his style, and of music in general at the time, was not quite etched in stone. The publication I have prepared here attempts to recreate as complete a picture as possible, and assimilates all variations into a written score, to give complete conception of the composer's intentions with integrity.

These arrangements draw on a maximum amount and variety of source materials. The 1950 manuscripts were primary sources, along with original manuscripts from the 1920's, which demonstrate his many variations. Other original manuscripts were found in Cuba. All the composer's recordings and piano rolls were consulted, particularly the piano roll of *La 32,* made years before the composer's recording, which had some wonderfully remarkable variants. The latter required laborious transcriptions by this author, both from scratchy 78-RPM disks and well-worn piano rolls. *Maullaba un Gato* has an entire section (the second half of the piece) which the composer never committed to paper, which I transcribed from the composer's recording. It is the most effective part of the work, but found only in this source. It is evident that Lecuona performed each piece through twice, with slight alterations in notes and rhythm the second time, something not alluded to in the manuscripts.

It is my sincere wish to aid the performer in not only understanding the works and how to perform them, but to give guidance and support for achieving these goals.

Thomas Y. Tirino

ANALYSIS: A GUIDE TO PERFORMANCE

Ni Tú, Ni Yo. "Neither you nor I." Pedaling in the opening section is Lecuona's and sets up the rhythmic feel. Play the middle section very *legato,* in a very assertive style to "declare the statement," and to give a different character between the two sections.

Measure 48, Lecuona takes a pause both times in his recording, something not found in the manuscript. I have saved it for the second statement, in *measure 106*.

Measures 53-58, Lecuona takes the passage down the octave in his recording, where as all manuscripts have it up the octave. For variation, I have left it the first time as it appears in the manuscript; the repeat, *measures 108-113*, has the passage down the octave, after the composer.

I suggest practicing the opening very slowly and very *legato* with accent on last beat of each measure to get the feel of the rhythm.

Mientras yo Comía, Maullaba un Gato. "While I was eating the cat meowed." A cat jumped up and began meowing at Lecuona during a whole meal while dining at a friend's house. He improvised this work that evening, imitating the event. Similarly, the piece must have an improvisatory feel, emulating cat "meowing," puttering walks, and cat's paw gestures. The opening right hand material must be played very *legato,* like cat "meows," suggested by the intervals. Slow *legato* practice of the right hand alone, with accents on the first beat should achieve this. Pedaling is Lecuona's and must be adhered to. The opening should be played as *piano* as possible.

Measure 7 makes a big *crescendo* to measure 8, giving the feel of a cat "snarl" with paw gesture, accenting well the downbeat of measure 8.

The middle section has pauses and hesitations in color and rhythm before downbeats, important in continuing the "meowing" feel, but with different character. The right hand melody must be *legatissimo* here. Lecuona's recording anticipates downbeats in this section, something not found in the manuscript. I have included these with their variants in different places, placing them at different points in the initial statement, and in the repeat.

Burlesca. The work should be playful, like the comical prankishness of a vaudeville act. Lecuona's *tempo* is very fast.

The opening section is to be played *leggiero,* while the middle section is angular, with strong off beat rhythmic accents, to suggest a ragtime or Joplin-like sound.

Measures 1-13. The left hand here is from Lecuona's recording. (No grace notes in right hand) The repeat in *measures 44-61* is from the manuscript.

Measures 31-44. The composer's pedaling. In the repeat in *measures 79-91*, the composer uses a longer pedal.

Practice the opening thirds with very high raised fingers *staccato* to achieve clarity, and the octaves of the middle section with a high wrist. Cascading figures after the octaves should be practiced very slowly and carefully; first *legato,* then *detaché* with raised fingers.

Mis Tristezas, "my sorrows" has a slow melancholic middle section expanding the form and suggesting its title. All pedaling is the composer's.

Lecuona's *tempo* is *prestissimo volante,* with octaves of the opening section *detaché.* Suggestions are very slow *staccato* practice, playing the melody *legatissimo* slowly, then *a tempo,* and repeating many times slowly, then quickly, accented leaps in the bass accompaniment with different rhythms. Use high raised fingers and wrist on each. These practice techniques should work well for the middle section as well.

The left-hand material, particularly in the middle section, differs considerably in the composer's recording and early manuscripts from later manuscripts. The original is used here with wide leaps, and changes of meter. The right hand of the middle section should be played *espressivo,* even in the fast speed. The slow *meno mosso* must express sorrow, *piu espressivo,* but **poco meno mosso,** so as not to create a third, sectionalized part of the piece, but rather an extension of the second half.

Measures 130-131, Lecuona brings out the left-hand melody in the repeat, which I have indicated.

Measures 139-140 in the repeat should be louder than in the opening.

El Miriñaque, must have the feel of rising and swaying up and down of a 19th century hoop dress. The semi-quaver phrases, and sudden *cresecendi* and *diminuendi* suggest this. The composer left no pedal marks, nor recording, so I have suggested pedaling to heighten this effect, with variants the second time (longer). The repeat of the middle should be played more *legato.* Dynamic marks and accents are Lecuona's.

La 32. Play very rapidly, with octaves in the opening *volante.* Practice them slowly *legatissimo,* then slowly *staccato* with a very high wrist on each.

Measures 6-7: The left hand here is from the composer's recording and piano roll, different from *measures 87-88,* which are from the manuscripts.

Measures 90-91: From the composer's piano roll.

Measure 99: The middle section in the repeat should be louder, which will set up the soft section following it.

Measures 115-130. Lecuona's recording suggests a *subito p* and *diminuendo* in the repeat to *pp*, differing from the manuscript, which has *forte*.

The bass in the middle section must be highly accented against a very light right hand. Practice *staccato*.

¡Cómo Baila el Muñeco! "How the male doll dances." Practice the leaps like those in *Mis Tristezas:* slowly, then *a tempo* with rhythmic accents, high wrists and fingers. I suggest adding pauses after leaps in slow practice to heighten awareness of the interval jumps.

The left hand and right hand chord additions differ in the composer's recording from the manuscripts: I used the recording material for the first half, and the manuscript material for the second half.

Measures 102-104 should be played *subito pp* the second time, setting up the *sfz* found in *measure 110.*

Measure 110: A *sfz* heightens the offbeat syncopation.

Measure 115-116. Lecuona's recording takes these two chords up the octave.

—T. Y. T.

SIETE DANZAS CUBANAS TIPICAS

I. Ni Tú, Ni Yo

ERNESTO LECUONA
arranged by Thomas Y. Tirino

Allegro moderato

Siete Danzas Cubanas Tipicas

Siete Danzas Cubanas Tipicas

Siete Danzas Cubanas Tipicas

Siete Danzas Cubanas Tipicas

Siete Danzas Cubanas Tipicas

II. Mientras yo Comía, Maullaba un Gato

ERNESTO LECUONA

arranged by Thomas Y. Tirino

Siete Danzas Cubanas Tipicas

Siete Danzas Cubanas Tipicas

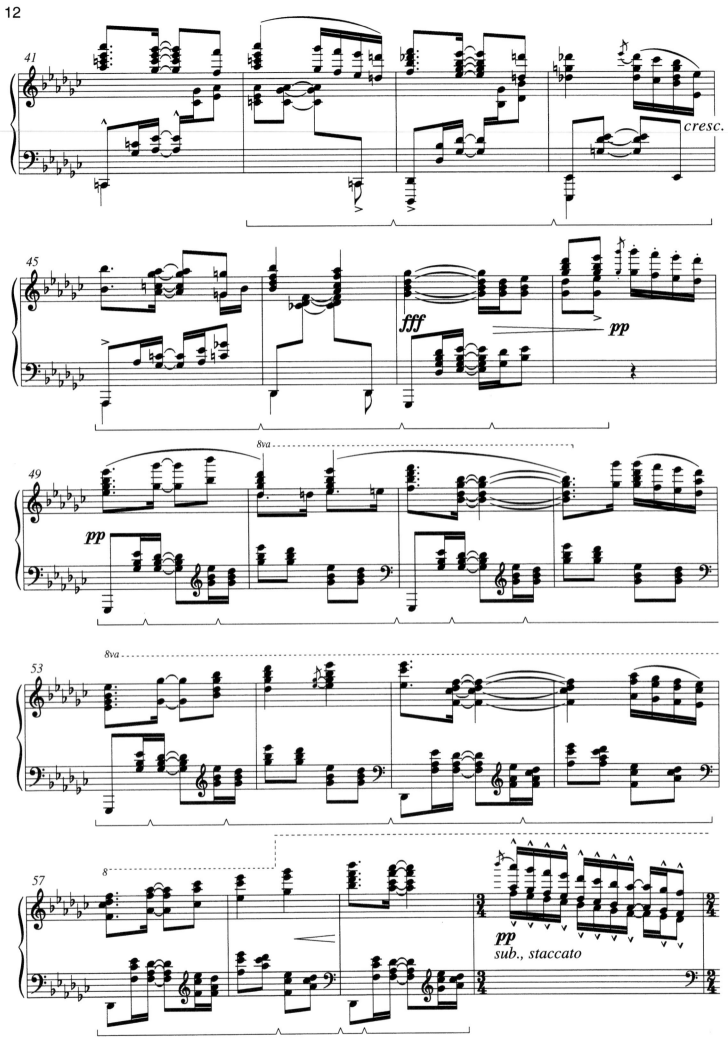

Siete Danzas Cubanas Tipicas

Siete Danzas Cubanas Tipicas

14

Siete Danzas Cubanas Tipicas

Siete Danzas Cubanas Tipicas

Siete Danzas Cubanas Tipicas

III. Burlesca

ERNESTO LECUONA
arranged by Thomas Y. Tirino

Allegro molto vivace

Siete Danzas Cubanas Tipicas

Siete Danzas Cubanas Tipicas

Siete Danzas Cubanas Tipicas

Siete Danzas Cubanas Tipicas

IV. Mis Tristezas

ERNESTO LECUONA
arranged by Thomas Y. Tirino

Allegro vivace

Siete Danzas Cubanas Tipicas

Siete Danzas Cubanas Tipicas

Siete Danzas Cubanas Tipicas

Siete Danzas Cubanas Tipicas

Siete Danzas Cubanas Tipicas

Siete Danzas Cubanas Tipicas

V. El Miriñaque

ERNESTO LECUONA
arranged by Thomas Y. Tirino

Allegro moderato

Siete Danzas Cubanas Tipicas

Siete Danzas Cubanas Tipicas

Siete Danzas Cubanas Tipicas

Siete Danzas Cubanas Tipicas

Siete Danzas Cubanas Tipicas

VI. La 32

ERNESTO LECUONA
arranged by Thomas Y. Tirino

Quasi presto

Siete Danzas Cubanas Tipicas

Siete Danzas Cubanas Tipicas

Siete Danzas Cubanas Tipicas

Siete Danzas Cubanas Tipicas

Siete Danzas Cubanas Tipicas

Siete Danzas Cubanas Tipicas

42

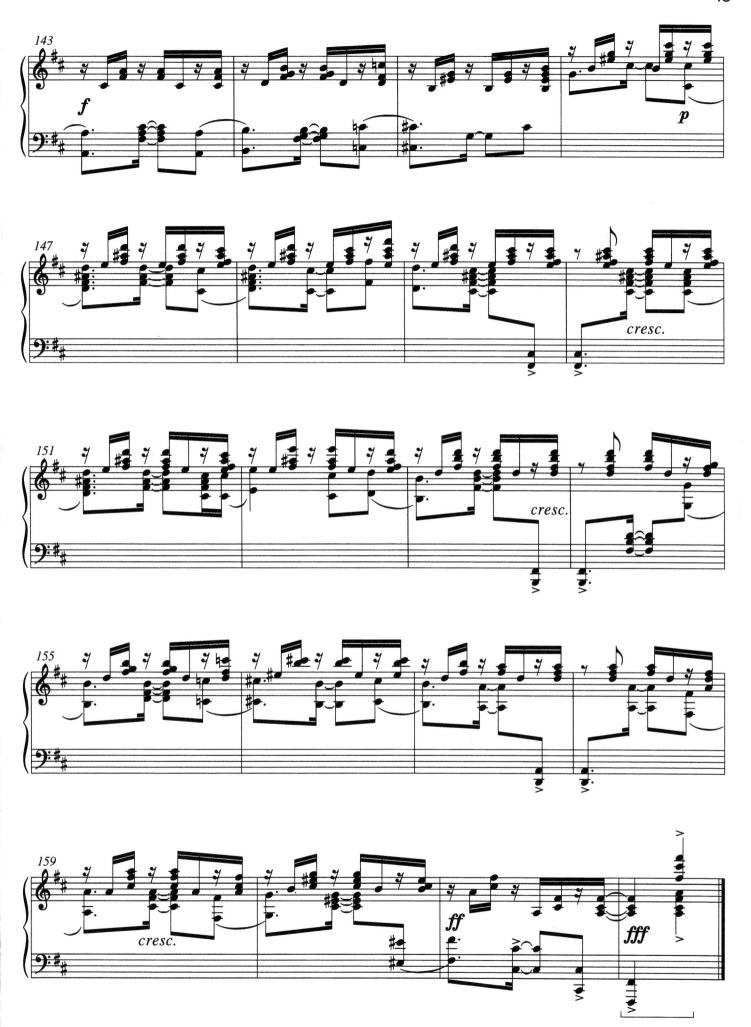

Siete Danzas Cubanas Tipicas

VII. ¡Cómo Baila el Muñeco!

ERNESTO LECUONA
arranged by Thomas Y. Tirino

Allegro molto

Siete Danzas Cubanas Tipicas

Siete Danzas Cubanas Tipicas

Siete Danzas Cubanas Tipicas

Siete Danzas Cubanas Tipicas